A Life Among Books

A Life Among Books

The Art of Collecting and Preserving the Printed Past

Andrew Norris

This book is intended for informational and educational purposes only. While every effort has been made to ensure accuracy, the author makes no guarantees regarding completeness or suitability for any particular purpose. Readers are encouraged to use their own judgment when making collecting or purchasing decisions.

First Edition.

ISBN: 979-8-9952514-0-8

Published by

Norris Bibliographic

Clayton, North Carolina, United States

Dedication:

For my family —

who give my time its meaning,

and for the books —

which give that time its memory.

"A room without books is like a body without a soul."

— Cicero

"The love of books is among the choicest gifts of the gods."

— Arthur Conan Doyle

"Books are the treasured wealth of the world and the fit inheritance of generations."

— Henry David Thoreau

Table of Contents

Introduction

On Care, Continuity, and the Things We Choose to Keep

I did not come to rare books through the trade, nor through academia or inheritance. I came to them gradually, by affection and by attention — the same way many meaningful pursuits enter a life.

My professional life is spent in family medicine and preventative care. Day after day, I am reminded that preservation matters more than repair — that small, consistent efforts shape long-term outcomes, and that what is cared for thoughtfully tends to endure. In medicine, this applies to people. In collecting, it applies to books.

Over time, the parallels became unmistakable.

A well-kept book, like a well-kept life, reflects foresight, stewardship, and respect for the future. Both reward patience. Both ask us to notice intricate details before they become large problems. Both receive help from measured judgment rather than haste.

Collecting rare books may seem distant from primary care, yet at heart they share a philosophy: we preserve what we value so that it may outlast us.

My love of books has found its place within my life as a
husband and father, not apart from it. Some of my happiest
moments as a collector have not been solitary acquisitions,
but shared discoveries — showing a child an illustration
that has survived a century, explaining how a book traveled
across time, or imagining who once turned these same
pages.

Books carry stories, but they also carry continuity. They
remind us that knowledge and imagination move across
generations the same way families do — through intent,
memory, and quiet transmission.

This manuscript was written not as a manual for
speculation, nor as a race toward high-value trophies, but
as an invitation to collect thoughtfully. To notice. To learn.
To enjoy the steady education of taste. To build a library
that reflects curiosity rather than fashion.

I write as a collector who continues to learn, still refining
my process and occasionally making mistakes that prove
instructive. If there is a central message in these pages, it is
this: Collecting favors attention over cleverness, patience
over haste, and genuine interest over strategy.

A meaningful library is not assembled in a season. It grows
alongside a life.

If this book helps you approach collecting with a little
more confidence, discernment, and joy, then it has done its
work.

And if, along the way, it encourages you to keep and care for the things that matter to you, whether books, knowledge, or family traditions, then it has done something even better.

We preserve what we love, and in doing so, we declare what we hope will endure.

CHAPTER I

Foundations of Collecting

The Nature of Rare-Book Collecting

Rare-book collecting stands at a unique crossroads where history, literature, and material culture meet — but it is also where private curiosity meets the enduring memory of the world.

A collectible book is never merely a vessel for text. It is a physical survivor of its era. Its paper has known different lights; its binding has rested in different rooms; its pages have been turned by readers whose lives are now finished, though their touch lingers faintly in the margins of time.

A softened corner, a penciled name, the gentle mellowing of paper — these are not imperfections alone, but evidence that a book has traveled. Each copy carries small, unrepeatable signs of passage, like the weathering of a well-walked path.

To collect books, then, is not simply to gather texts. It is to notice these survivals and to value them. It is to recognize that an object made decades or centuries ago has arrived intact enough to be held, opened and read again.

Collectors become not only readers, but custodians — temporary guardians of objects that predate them and may well outlast them. There is a subtle humility in this role. One does not so much possess a rare book as receive it for a time.

Seen this way, collecting shifts from acquisition to care. The collector enters a longer story already in progress and agrees to carry it forward.

Every rare book, in its way, is a message that time chose not to erase.

Rarity and Desirability

One of the earliest revelations in collecting is that rarity alone does not create value.

Scarcity can exist silently. A book may be rare simply because few people thought to keep it. Time washes many things without necessarily granting them importance.

Desirability, by contrast, is animated by human interest. It arises when a book continues to matter — when readers return to it, collectors seek it, and culture remembers it.

The market keeps its finger firmly on the pulse of this distinction.

A slender theological pamphlet printed in a run of one hundred copies may be genuinely scarce today. Yet if its author is obscure and its subject no longer speaks to contemporary curiosity, it may rest in relative silence.

Meanwhile, a beloved children's classic printed in the thousands may remain in steady demand because it lives vividly in memory. Stories carried through childhood regularly travel into adulthood, and the books that held them maintain lasting emotional gravity.

Collectors eventually learn that rarity and desirability do not always walk together. One measures quantity of survival, the other measures significance.

Value emerges where the two meet.

There is also a human truth beneath the economics: people pursue what moves them. A book that shaped imagination or thought will be sought long after a merely scarce one is forgotten.

A useful rule of thumb circulates among seasoned collectors:

If only ten copies exist but only three people care, the market is still. If thousands exist and thousands care, the market is lively.

Desire, more than scarcity, creates energy.

To recognize this is not to diminish rarity, but to understand it in context. Rarity becomes meaningful when it intersects with memory, influence, and cultural presence.

Collectors who grasp this early save themselves both disappointment and confusion. They begin to look not only at how many copies survive, but at why the book still matters.

Scarcity preserves a book; significance preserves its audience.

Condition as a Pillar of Value

Condition is one of the primary drivers of value in rare books, but it is also something more reflective than a simple grade.

It is the visible record of a book's survival.

Two copies of the same edition may share identical text and printing history, yet live very different physical lives. One may have rested on careful shelves; another may have traveled through attics, trunks, or frequent handling. Their differences are not merely cosmetic — they are biographical.

Condition tells the story of how a book has weathered time. Yet it must always be understood in context. A book is not judged against perfection, but against its era.

Collectors learn to weigh condition alongside the age of the book, the materials from which it was made, the typical survival state for its period, and the ways such books were historically used.

An eighteenth-century volume in Very Good condition may be remarkable.

A twentieth-century book in the same state may be ordinary.

Perspective protects the collector from unrealistic expectations. A 250-year-old book is allowed to look 250 years old. Indeed, a copy of the same book that appears unnaturally pristine invites closer examination.

There is wisdom in accepting that honest signs of age are not failures of preservation but evidence of real survival.

Light foxing, gentle rubbing, or a tactful inscription can reflect a life lived carefully rather than a life neglected.

In this sense, condition becomes less about perfection and more about proportion. The attentive collector asks not "Is it perfect?" but "Is it appropriate?"

This shift in thinking marks a turning point in collecting maturity. Time leaves its signature on every book; the fortunate ones bear it lightly.

When Condition Meets the Market

High-end auctions offer the clearest lessons in how profoundly condition shapes value.

Consider the market for early printings of *The Great Gatsby* (1925) by F. Scott Fitzgerald — a book neither obscure nor vanishingly rare in absolute numbers. Several hundred copies are believed to survive. Yet the prices realized for individual copies can vary dramatically.

The explanation lies not in the text, which is identical, but in preservation.

Imagine two copies appearing in different auctions.

One shows the honest fatigue of its age: cloth slightly worn, spine a bit dulled, a dust jacket chipped at the edges and price-clipped long ago. The pages are clean but faintly toned, the structure sound but softened. It is, by all reasonable standards, a respectable copy — one that has clearly lived a careful life. It attracts interest and commands a substantial price, as any early *Gatsby* will. Yet it settles into the mid-range of results.

Now consider another. Its cloth remains bright, its lettering crisp. The dust jacket survives unrestored, with its price intact, the colors still lively after a century. The pages are fresh, the hinges firm, the whole volume carrying an air of improbable preservation.

When such a copy appears, the room feels different. Bidding stretches and outpaces estimation. Collectors recognize that they are not merely competing for the book, but for a version of it that time has failed to capture in its inevitable embrace.

The price realized may be many multiples of the first copy. Not because the words differ. Not because the edition changes. But because survival has.

At this level, small differences become enormous distinctions. Originality, eye appeal, and structural integrity take on amplified importance. Dust jackets, once considered disposable, become decisive.

The market, in these moments, reveals a simple truth: collectors pursue not only titles, but examples — specific survivors that carry their history.

In rare books, condition does not change the story printed on the page, but it changes the story the book itself can tell.

Honest Wear and True Damage

Collectors learn to distinguish between the marks of time and the marks of neglect.

The difference is subtle but meaningful.

Honest wear is the evidence of a book that has lived carefully. It may show itself as light foxing, gentle rubbing to the boards, or a discreet owner's inscription placed with intention. These signs speak of use, but also of regard. They suggest the book was read, kept, and considered worth preserving.

True damage tells a different story. Water exposure, missing pages, crude repairs, or careless handling reflect not the passage of years but the absence of care. Such harm interrupts the book's continuity and, at times, its integrity.

Time, when paired with respect, leaves a softer trace.

Collecting as Stewardship

With time, many collectors come to see their libraries differently. What begins as acquisition gradually becomes guardianship.

A valued book may cross decades or centuries through the decisions of people who chose, at some point, to keep it safe. To collect such objects is to enter this honorable chain of preservation.

The role carries an understated responsibility. Books are vulnerable to light, moisture, neglect, and haste. Their continued life depends less on admiration than on attentiveness. Proper storage, careful handling, and thoughtful documentation are small acts, but they accumulate into longevity.

Stewardship is not a burden; it is a privilege. The collector becomes a temporary caretaker of something that does not belong entirely to any one lifetime. This perspective influences how books are chosen. One begins to ask not only "Do I want this?" but also "Can I care for this well?" The question is subtle, but it reflects the development of collecting wisely. Collectors who think this way rarely treat books as trophies. They treat them as inheritances received early.

And in time, every collector becomes a predecessor. The books will move on — to other shelves, other hands, other readers. Their journey continues whether we witness it or not.

And the finest collectors are remembered not for what they held, but for what they preserved

CHAPTER II

Understanding Condition

The Language of Condition

Condition is the grammar of rare-book collecting.

It is the shared language through which collectors, dealers, and auction houses describe the physical life of a book. Yet, like any language, it demands interpretation. Words alone rarely tell the full story.

A single term — *Very Good, Near Fine, Good* — may conceal a wide spectrum of realities. No grade exists apart from context, and no description replaces the evidence of the eye and hand.

To understand condition is not merely to memorize terminology, but to learn how books age, how they were used, and how they endure. It is to recognize that every book carries a physical history alongside its printed one.

Seeing the Book as an Object

Before a book is literature, it is structure.

Paper, cloth, boards, glue, and thread form the delicate engineering that allows a text to survive generations. These elements do their work in the background, yet they determine whether a book remains sound or slowly fails.

Collectors who learn to see the book as an object develop steadier judgment than those who look only at the title page.

When assessing condition, structure deserves the first glance.

A firm spine, secure hinges, and well-attached boards suggest stability. A book may appear attractive on the surface yet conceal weakness beneath. Cosmetic charm cannot compensate for structural compromise.

A book, after all, is built to hold together for reading — and its integrity is part of its story.

But structure is not only about durability; it is also about intention. The way a book was made reveals how it was meant to be used. A cheaply bound volume signals different expectations than a finely sewn text block. Materials speak, if one learns their language.

Sewn bindings, for example, tend to flex and prevail. Adhesive bindings, while common in modern books, may become brittle with time. Endpapers that are cracked or split tell of repeated opening, sometimes careful, sometimes hurried. None of these are moral failings of a book — they are simply evidence of how it has been handled and how it was constructed.

Even the boards themselves offer clues. Warping may suggest fluctuations in humidity. Loose boards may point to strain at the joints. A text block that leans indicates long periods shelved without support. These observations are not advanced techniques; they are habits of attention.

Experienced collectors develop a steady routine: lifting a book gently, feeling its balance, opening it just enough to sense the binding's response. The book answers with modest measure. A healthy binding moves with ease. A compromised one resists.

Over time, this awareness becomes intuitive. One no longer inspects a book only with the eyes, but with the hands, the ears, and with other senses. Judgment grows not from suspicion, but from familiarity.

To see the book as an object is not to reduce it to mechanics. It is to recognize that the physical form is what allows the text to persist at all. Without structure, the ideas within would have little chance of surviving use.

A collector who understands this does not handle books timidly, but attentively. Respect for structure leads naturally to better care, better storage, and wiser purchasing decisions.

The most satisfying copies are not those that look impressive at a glance, but those that are sound where it matters most.

A Small Habit Worth Forming

Seasoned collectors open a book gently and observe how it responds.

A sound binding yields with supple flexibility. A compromised one resists, cracks, or separates. The difference can be felt before it is seen.

This simple gesture, performed carefully, reveals much in moments. Books speak softly, but they do speak.

The value of this habit lies not in diagnosis, but in consideration. It encourages a pause before judgment. Rather than rushing to impressions formed by a jacket or a reputation, the collector begins with a quiet introduction to the book itself.

Many disappointments in collecting arise from haste — a purchase made on enthusiasm alone, a listing trusted too quickly, a detail overlooked in eagerness. The small ritual of opening a book slowly helps temper that impulse. It invites the collector to meet the book on its own terms.

Over time, this practice cultivates sensitivity. The hands learn what the eyes might miss. A slight stiffness, an unexpected looseness, a subtle unevenness — these impressions accumulate into experience. They cannot be memorized from guides; they must be felt.

There is also something humanizing in this gesture. To open a book with care is to acknowledge that it has had a life before arriving in your hands. The moment becomes less transactional and more observational, almost conversational.

No special expertise is required. Only patience.

With repetition, the act becomes second nature. The collector no longer thinks, "I must inspect this," but simply interacts with the book in a measured way.

A small habit, practiced consistently, can shape a collector's judgment more than grand strategies ever will.

Paper as Witness

Paper remembers. It records light, air, handling, and time. It yellows, softens, freckles, and stains. These changes are not merely flaws; they are the visible biography of the object.

Foxing — those familiar rust-colored specks — is among the most misunderstood features in older books. Light foxing is common in 18th- and 19th-century volumes and reflects storage conditions more than disrepair.

Heavy foxing that obscures text or accompanies moisture damage is another matter. Here, the paper tells a different story. As with all things in collecting, proportion matters more than purity.

Paper also varies greatly by era. Earlier rag papers, made from linen and cotton fibers, were remarkably durable. Many survive today with a strength that surprises those accustomed to modern wood-pulp sheets. By contrast, late 19th- and early 20th-century acidic papers often grow brittle, even when they appear visually clean. A page that snaps at the corner reveals as much about its composition as its care.

Edges provide further clues. Darkened margins may show where a book sat exposed on a shelf. Uneven toning can indicate how it rested when stored. A faint tide mark may trace a long-ago encounter with moisture. None of these

signs automatically diminish a book; they simply describe
its environmental history.

Texture, too, offers information. Some papers retain a
pleasing firmness; others become thin and delicate. A
collector who turns pages slowly can feel this difference
immediately. One learns, over time, which papers invite
confidence and which require greater caution.

Pristine paper in a very old book can raise questions. A text
block that appears unnaturally bright may have been
washed or treated. Such processes are not inherently
misguided, but they do alter the book's material history and
should be understood for what they are. To read paper well
is to read evidence. The page holds a record not only of
printing, but of environment, storage, and use. A careful
observer can learn where a book has been simply by
studying the leaves.

Paper, in this sense, is less a passive surface than an archive
in its own right.

The Collector's Nose

Experienced collectors may admit, with a hint of
embarrassment, that they smell books.

A faintly sweet, dry scent occasionally accompanies well-
aged paper — the slow chemistry of aging fibers at work. A

sharp musty odor may signal past moisture, even when stains are faint.

This is not romanticism; it is observation. The senses perceive what the eye has yet to confirm. Books, like old houses, carry the atmosphere of their history.

Certain smells offer useful clues. A persistent mildew scent may indicate storage in a damp cellar or poorly ventilated room. A smoky trace can suggest long residence near fireplaces or in rooms where tobacco was common. Occasionally, a book carries the neutral dryness of stable storage — a reassuring sign for many collectors.

Bindings contribute their own notes. Leather can produce a warm, slightly earthy aroma, particularly in older calf or goatskin. Cloth bindings tend to hold environmental odors more readily, absorbing the character of the spaces they have occupied. Even adhesives, in some modern volumes, release faint chemical traces as they age.

None of these scents automatically condemn a book. They are simply part of its material reality. What matters is whether the odor is stable or active. A book that smells strongly of dampness today may still be reacting to moisture exposure; one with a faint residual scent may merely carry a memory of earlier conditions.

Collectors who cultivate this sense do not rely on it alone, but they rarely ignore it. Smell can prompt a closer look at hinges, endpapers, or page edges. It acts as an early signal rather than a final judgment.

There is also a practical reason for this awareness. Books stored in poor environments may affect neighboring volumes. Identifying a problematic copy early can prevent wider issues within a collection.

Over time, familiarity builds. What once seemed indistinguishable becomes readable. A collector may not describe these impressions in technical language, but they recognize them when encountered.

In this way, the nose becomes another instrument of evaluation — not mystical, not sentimental, simply informed by experience.

Marks of Ownership

Not all writing is vandalism. A discreet inscription, a period signature, or light pencil notes can lend character and, at times, historical interest. They remind us that books were made to be read, given, and kept.

Context governs interpretation. An author's inscription may transform a copy. A child's crayon rarely does.

Collectors learn to distinguish intrusion from trace. The former distracts; the latter documents.

Books that have lived careful lives bear small, human signatures of use — inconspicuous evidence that they once mattered to someone else.

Dates written on a flyleaf can be surprisingly informative. A gift inscription from 1897 anchors a book to a moment in time and place, confirming how quickly it circulated after publication. A school prize label pasted inside a Victorian volume can reveal how books moved through academic settings and social customs.

Signatures also tell their own stories. A simple name in iron gall ink, written in a practiced hand, may reflect ownership when penmanship was a point of pride. By contrast, a hurried ballpoint signature in a much older book can signal later handling and may hold less interpretive value.

Marginal notes deserve careful reading. Some merely summarize passages; others debate the author, correct errors, or highlight passages that struck a prior reader as important. In theological works, legal texts, and scientific treatises, such notes illuminate how the book was actually used.

Books from institutional libraries introduce another layer. Discard stamps, shelf numbers, and bookplates from monasteries, private schools, or subscription libraries can document a book's movement through organized collections. Some collectors avoid these marks; others find them appealing as part of the book's journey through formal settings.

Even something as modest as a bookseller's pencil price on the endpaper can interest certain collectors, especially when it comes from a respected historical dealer. It records a moment in the book trade itself.

Of course, not every mark enhances desirability. Heavy underlining, intrusive annotations in ink, or modern highlighter distract from the text. The distinction lies not in the mere presence of marks, but in their relevance and restraint.

Experienced collectors evaluate these signs individually. A well-placed inscription can enrich a copy; excessive marking can overwhelm it. Between those extremes lies a wide and nuanced middle ground.

Ownership marks, when read carefully, reveal patterns of readership, education, and taste. They are small records of how books moved through ordinary lives — and how readers once engaged with them.

The Curious Case of Dust Jackets

Dust jackets, once treated as disposable wrappers, now hold a peculiar authority in modern collecting.

For many 20th-century first editions, the jacket represents a significant portion of value. It is both protection and artifact — a piece of the book's original presentation.

A worn but authentic jacket is generally preferred to a flawless facsimile. Authenticity, even when imperfect, carries weight.

A chipped original still speaks in the voice of its era. A replacement, however skillful, speaks in ours.

Collectors, when given the choice, tend to listen for the earlier voice.

Part of this preference stems from history. Early dust jackets were meant to be discarded once the book reached its owner. They bore prices, advertisements, and design elements tied to the moment of publication. Because many were thrown away, survivors now offer a glimpse into how a book first appeared in the marketplace.

Design matters here. The color palette, typography, and even the blurbs chosen by the publisher reveal how the book was positioned to readers. A jacket designed by a known illustrator — such as the iconic artwork on mid-century fiction — can become as recognizable as the text itself.

Price-clipping introduces another nuance. A clipped corner does not always signal damage; it indicates the book was given as a gift. Still, an unclipped jacket commands a premium, since it preserves the book exactly as it left the publisher.

Condition standards for jackets also differ from those for books. Small chips, short tears, or gentle creasing are common and typically tolerated, particularly when the rest of the jacket remains presentable. What matters most is completeness and overall appearance.

Protective covers have become standard practice for this reason. Clear archival sleeves now guard jackets from further wear while allowing them to be viewed. This modern intervention aims not to alter the jacket, but to slow additional damage.

It is also worth noting that facsimile jackets have their place. They can improve presentation for reading copies or fill gaps in personal libraries. Problems arise only when reproductions are mistaken for originals. Transparency remains essential.

Ultimately, the dust jacket reminds collectors that books were once commercial objects as well as literary ones. The wrapper reflects how a publisher introduced the work to the world — what was emphasized, how it was marketed, and how it was expected to appeal.

Restoration: A Delicate Subject

Restoration occupies a careful middle ground between preservation and alteration.

A sympathetic repair may extend a book's life. A cleaned page may restore legibility. Such work is not inherently wrong; it reflects respect for the object.

Yet restoration alters originality. Collectors value transparency. An undisclosed repair distorts trust more than the repair itself. Knowledge allows judgment; concealment disrupts it. A book that appears improbably fresh for its age invites a second look. Time leaves traces, and their absence can be as telling as their presence.

Not all restoration is equal. Some interventions stabilize a book without materially changing its character. Others reshape appearance more dramatically. Reattaching a loose hinge differs from replacing endpapers; mending a tear differs from washing an entire text block.

Professional conservation typically aims to preserve as much original material as possible. The goal is stability and usability rather than visual perfection. In this approach, repairs are reversible and documented.

Commercial restoration prioritizes appearance. Re-backed spines, recolored cloth, or skillful infilling can make a book look markedly improved. When disclosed, such work may be acceptable to many buyers. When hidden, it raises understandable concern.

Market response varies by category. In early printed books, careful conservation is widely accepted because survival depends on it. In modern first editions, heavy restoration may reduce desirability, since collectors generally prefer untouched examples when available.

There are also gray areas. A replaced dust jacket spine panel, for instance, might improve display while reducing originality. A trimmed margin may remove damage yet alter format. Each case invites individual evaluation.

Experienced collectors ask simple questions:

What was done?

Who performed the work?

Is it visible?

Is it documented?

Clear answers build confidence.

Restoration, at its best, allows a book to remain usable and intact. At its worst, it attempts to disguise reality. The distinction lies less in the act itself than in the honesty surrounding it. Informed buyers rarely demand flawlessness. They seek clarity.

A Balanced Perspective

Perfection is rare in antiquarian books.

Survival, not flawlessness, is the rule. A book that has traveled two centuries to reach your hands has already endured shifting climates, changing tastes, and human handling.

The collector's task is not to find untouched relics, but to recognize well-preserved survivors.

Books age, as people do. A few lines add character; too many tell of harder trials.

CHAPTER III

Evaluating Listings and Dealers

The Book Before the Book

Condition teaches us how to read the book itself. The marketplace teaches us how to read those who describe it.

In modern collecting, one frequently encounters a book first as a description.

A listing, a catalog entry, an auction lot — these are the gateways through which books reach collectors. Before the volume is held, it is translated into language and images.

Learning to read these representations carefully is part of the collector's education.

A listing reflects what the seller chose to emphasize, what they noticed, and what they did not.

To read a listing well is to read between lines as well as within them.

The Role of the Seller

A good bookseller is not merely a vendor but a guide.

The rare-book trade has long depended on reputation, continuity, and trust. Many dealers spend years cultivating accuracy because their livelihood — and their standing among collectors — depends upon it.

It is also worth remembering that many sellers are collectors themselves. They entered the trade not solely for commerce, but also due to fascination. Their shelves mirror their own personal curiosities as well as the interests of their customers, and their knowledge is frequently born of independent pursuit rather than mere inventory.

Such sellers take genuine pleasure in discussion. A thoughtful question about a book's history, binding, or provenance is rarely an intrusion; it is an invitation to share what they know. Conversations about books tend to be one of the simple joys of the trade.

Collectors benefit from approaching sellers neither with blind faith nor reflexive suspicion, but with measured respect and curiosity. A thoughtful seller appreciates an inquisitive buyer.

In the best cases, the relationship becomes collegial rather than transactional — a meeting of shared interests rather than a simple exchange of goods. Collegial relationships shape the bonds of trust that develop into future conversations and purchases.

Many collectors can trace part of their education to a revealing conversation in a bookshop. Such moments are easily overlooked, yet they form part of how collectors are slowly made. The trade, at its finest, is sustained not only by commerce, but by honest conversation and shared passion.

In the end, many collectors discover their finest acquisitions were not books at all, but the knowledge and understanding gathered along the way.

Long after prices and purchases fade from memory, it is these small exchanges that remain, like pressed leaves between the pages of one's collecting life.

The Language of Description

Bookseller language is its own dialect.

It has evolved through decades of catalogs, fairs, and correspondence. Certain phrases recur not because they are evasive, but because they compress meaning into familiar shorthand.

A "nice copy" suggests an attractive example with minor imperfections.

"Sound but worn" typically signals structural stability with cosmetic age.

"Sympathetically restored" implies repairs made with restraint.

These are not codes so much as conventions.

Over time, collectors learn to hear the tone behind the words. A sparse description may indicate efficiency — or limited inspection. A detailed one may reflect care.

Specificity usually signals confidence.

Photographs as Evidence

Photographs have become the modern surrogate for handling.

A thorough listing typically shows the spine, boards, title page, and any notable flaws. When these views are absent, it is not inherently suspicious, but it may justify inquiry.

Images, like descriptions, are selective. They illuminate what is shown and conceal what is not.

Collectors gradually develop an eye for what angles reveal: the tilt of a spine, the sharpness of corners, the brightness of cloth.

A photograph rarely lies, but it does not always tell the whole story.

The Art of Asking

Questions need not be confrontational to be useful.

"Are the hinges secure?"

"Is there any restoration?"

"Are all plates present?"

Such inquiries signal seriousness. Reputable sellers generally respond candidly.

The tone of the exchange reveals as much as the answer itself. Courtesy tends to invite candor. The rare-book world remains, in many respects, a small and conversational arena.

Reputation and Continuity

Longevity in the trade matters.

A dealer who has described books for decades develops habits of accuracy. A firm known for bibliographic detail rarely benefits from carelessness.

This does not make them infallible, but it does provide context.

Collectors, like scholars, learn to notice patterns. A seller's consistency eventually becomes its own credential.

Dealers and Auctions: Two Voices

Dealers and auction houses speak in slightly different tones.

Dealers generally provide richer narrative description. Auctions may offer fewer words but more images. One emphasizes interpretation, the other documentation.

Neither is inherently superior. Each requires a slightly different reading.

Collectors learn to listen to both voices.

A Gentle Perspective

Most misunderstandings arise not from deception, but from differing expectations.

A book described as "very good" by one seller may appear merely "good" to another. Human judgment enters every description.

Experienced collectors allow for this margin. They read listings as informed approximations, not as legal contracts.

"Condition grades are opinions with footnotes." The remark carries more wisdom than cynicism.

Part of the challenge lies in language itself. Terms such as *fine*, *very good*, or *good* carry shared conventions, yet they remain elastic. Two honest professionals may apply the same term to copies that differ noticeably. Lighting, photography, and even screen settings can further influence perception.

Descriptions also reflect a seller's experience. A dealer who handles high-end material daily may apply stricter standards than one who sells more general stock. Neither is necessarily wrong; they operate within different frames of reference.

For this reason, detailed notes may matter more than the headline grade. Specific mentions of rubbing, foxing, repairs, or wear provide clearer guidance than a single adjective. Collectors who focus on the details rather than the summary usually make sounder decisions.

It is also worth remembering that sellers are describing objects, not making promises about personal satisfaction. One buyer may accept a flaw that another would find distracting. The final judgment always rests with the individual collector.

Over time, patterns become familiar. A collector learns which sellers describe conservatively, which photograph generously, and which provide thorough detail. This knowledge comes from experience rather than rules.

Patience plays a role here. The urge to secure a desired title quickly can magnify small uncertainties. Taking a moment to read carefully, compare examples, or request clarification frequently leads to greater confidence.

In the end, condition language functions as a shared shorthand, not a precise measurement. It guides expectations but does not replace direct evaluation.

Collectors who approach descriptions with flexibility tend to encounter fewer disappointments and more satisfying acquisitions.

To evaluate listings well is to cultivate attentiveness.

The careful collector reads a description the way one reads a preface — thoughtfully, alert to nuance, aware that words are guides but not substitutes for the object itself.

In time, patterns emerge. Judgment sharpens. Confidence grows.

And the collector learns that every listing is not merely a sales pitch, but an invitation to look more closely.

CHAPTER IV

On Auctions and the Temperament of Bidding

The Character of Auctions

Auctions possess a peculiar atmosphere.

Even in their digital form, they retain something of the theater from which they descend. There is anticipation, pacing, and the subtle electricity of competition. A bid placed in the final seconds can feel momentous, though the object itself has waited decades — possibly centuries — to be summoned to the block again.

Auction rooms, whether physical or virtual, carry their own measured choreography: the calibrated cadence of the auctioneer, the muted murmur of the room, the restrained rustle of catalogs turning. Time seems to compress and stretch at once.

For the uninitiated, auctions can feel exhilarating. For the seasoned collector, they are exercises in composure.

The difference lies not in knowledge, but in temperament.

Auctions are arenas of possibility and pressure, where patience contends with impulse and prudence competes with pride. The environment invites quick decisions yet rewards careful considerations.

There is an eccentric poetry in the process — a ritual of raised paddles, recorded bids, and resolute silences. Objects that have slept on shelves for generations suddenly stand at the center of attention; their worth weighed in increments, and with intention.

And yet, beneath the drama, the truth remains simple: the book is unchanged by the bidding. It is only the buyers who are stirred.

The seasoned collector learns to watch the rhythm without being swept into the rush.

The Price Behind the Price

The hammer price is only the beginning of the story.

Buyer's premiums, taxes, shipping, and currency conversions gather inconspicuously in the background. A book that seemed modestly priced may reveal its true cost only after the arithmetic is complete.

Experienced collectors perform this calculation before they bid, not after they win.

It is a small habit, but a protective one.

Some keep a private rule: If the final cost would trouble you tomorrow, it should trouble you today.

Auctions favor clarity over optimism.

Premium structures vary widely. Some houses charge a flat percentage; others use tiered rates that increase or decrease at certain thresholds. The difference between twenty and twenty-eight percent can be meaningful on higher lots.

Taxes introduce another layer. Local regulations, import duties, and use taxes apply depending on location. International purchases can carry additional charges that appear only once a shipment crosses a border.

Shipping also deserves scrutiny. A large or fragile volume may require specialized packing, insurance, or courier services. These costs are justified but easily underestimated by new bidders.

Currency conversion can introduce subtle surprises. Exchange rates shift daily, and credit card providers add foreign transaction fees. A favorable rate at the time of bidding may look different by the time the statement arrives.

Catalog estimates, meanwhile, reflect guidance rather than guarantees. They provide a range based on prior sales and market knowledge, but bidding frequently exceeds them. A low estimate does not mean a low final price.

For this reason, many seasoned buyers set a personal ceiling that already includes premiums and expected charges. Once reached, they stop — regardless of how appealing the lot remains.

Written notes can help. Some collectors jot their all-in maximum beside each lot before the sale begins. This removes guesswork in the moment and keeps decisions grounded in preparation rather than excitement.

None of this diminishes the enjoyment of auctions. It simply ensures that enthusiasm is paired with awareness.

The Matter of Limits

A maximum bid is best decided in calm air, not competitive heat.

It reflects research, condition, rarity, and personal comfort. Once set, it becomes a tacit contract within oneself.

The temptation to stretch "just a little further" is familiar to everyone who has ever bid in earnest. Yet auctions have a way of testing resolve with incremental persistence. The collector who exceeds a reasonable limit rehearses the moment again, wondering where restraint might have entered the equation.

Discipline rarely feels dramatic, but it ages well.

Another copy generally appears. Not always quickly, not always identical, but frequently enough to justify patience. Books have a way of resurfacing with patience.

Emotional Bidding

Auctions are designed to awaken urgency. A book can appear suddenly singular simply because another bidder desires it. Competition lends importance; importance lends attachment.

It is easy to forget, in the rhythm of rising bids, that one is purchasing an object rather than winning a contest. Auctions can blur this distinction.

Seasoned collectors learn to notice the quickening pulse without obeying it. They remember that they are acquiring an artifact, not securing a victory.

The Myth of the Last Chance

Auction descriptions murmur of rarity: *unlikely to appear again, the only copy seen in years, a fleeting opportunity.*

Such phrases have a way of settling into the collector's mind. They awaken the lingering fear of absence — the sense that a door may be closing.

It is a familiar feeling: the quickened pulse, the inner calculation, the subtle persuasion that this moment must not be missed.

Yet the rare-book world moves in longer rhythms than our anticipations. Libraries are dispersed, estates are settled, collections are gradually reshaped by time. Books migrate across generations and geographies with surprising patience.

What disappears today re-emerges tomorrow — in another catalog, another city, another season.

Many experienced collectors can recall a book they once let pass, convinced it would never return, only to encounter it again years later under calmer circumstances and kinder terms. They also recall the books they chased too urgently, where the memory of the chase outlasted the pleasure of ownership.

Time, in collecting, is rarely an adversary. More frequently, it is an ally to those who allow it to work.

The notion of a "last chance" is seductive because it flatters urgency. But books, unlike moments, are built to endure. They wait on shelves, in estates, in the tucked-away corners of shops, patient beyond our immediate desires.

Patience, in this sphere, is not resignation. It is confidence in the long life of books. A book that has survived a century can usually survive your decision to wait another season.

The Value of Records

Many experienced collectors keep personal notes on past results.

Not elaborate ledgers — simply remembered comparisons, occasional records, mental markers. With time, these impressions form a private compass.

Experience does not arrive fully formed. It gathers gradually, like marginalia in the mind.

Patterns emerge for those who pay attention.

CHAPTER V

Provenance and Value

The Lives a Book Has Lived

Every old book has lived more than one life.

Before it arrives on a collector's shelf, it has already inhabited other rooms, rested on other night tables, traveled through other seasons of someone else's days. It has been opened in curiosity, consulted in study, possibly gifted in affection, perhaps packed away during moves and rediscovered years later.

Few old books survive by accident alone. Someone, at some point, chose to keep it.

Provenance is the faint record of these choices. It is the partial biography of an object that has outlived its first context and, regularly, its original readers.

The traces are visible: a name, a date, a bookplate. They are implied by survival itself. A volume that endured wars, relocations, estate clearings, and changing tastes has already passed through many thresholds.

One can imagine such a book resting in lamplight a century ago, its pages turned by someone whose concerns and hopes were as immediate to them as ours are now. The book that feels old to us may once have felt entirely new to them.

This is part of provenance's gentle power. It reminds us that books are not only artifacts of printing, but companions in living. They witness more than they reveal.

A book that has passed through generations does not belong entirely to any one of them. It carries forward fragments of many lives, most of which will never be fully known.

And yet, their presence is faintly felt in the margins of survival. Every old book is, in modest degree, a survivor of other people's ordinary days.

Marks of Passage

Provenance rarely announces itself proudly. Characteristically, it may whisper from a flyleaf, a bookplate, or a careful inscription left for another age.

A bookplate may rest on the pastedown, its edges gently toned by decades of air. Turn a page and a dated signature emerges, the ink mellowed to brown. Elsewhere, a bookseller's ticket recalls a shop whose windows no longer light any street. Even a penciled price, once purely practical, can read like a small historical footnote.

These are not blemishes. They are traces of custody.

Each mark suggests a moment when the book mattered enough to be claimed, recorded, or remembered. A name written carefully inside a cover is rarely casual; it is a small declaration of belonging.

Such marks remind us that books were not created for glass cases. They were held, read, loaned, packed into boxes, placed on shelves beside other favorites.

Some inscriptions are formal, others affectionate. A holiday gift dated in December. A school prize recorded in careful script. A brief line wishing enjoyment to a future reader. These fragments of handwriting carry an enduring intimacy across decades.

Even the humblest notation can humanize a book. It suggests that someone once paused, pen in hand, and felt the object was worth claiming.

Collectors debate whether such traces enhance or diminish desirability. Yet beyond markets and grades, these marks perform a subtler function: they remind us that a book has been part of lived experience.

They are the fingerprints of readership.

Not all histories survive in archives. In these small inscriptions and faded labels, a book remembers the hands that history forgot.

When Provenance Deepens Value

Not all provenance proves meaningful, yet some provenance possesses poignant power.

When a book can be placed meaningfully in the orbit of history — in the hands of an author, a statesman, a scholar, or a notable collector — it gains a dimension beyond its printing. It becomes not only an artifact of publication, but a witness to a life.

Yet the power of provenance lies not merely in fame, but in relevance. A celebrated name loosely connected to a book may intrigue; a meaningful connection can resonate.

For example, a signed first edition of *Watership Down* by Richard Adams becomes more than a desirable modern first when inscribed to Alan Aldridge, the illustrator who later collaborated with Adams and helped shape the visual imagination surrounding his work. The association is not incidental; it reflects a genuine creative relationship between author and artist, text and image.

In such a case, the inscription does more than display a signature — it documents a connection within the book's own creative orbit. The provenance aligns naturally with the work itself, deepening its narrative.

Collectors sense the difference intuitively. They respond not only to who owned a book, but why the connection might have mattered to them.

An author's copy of their own work, annotated in their hand, feels alive in a way a random signature cannot. A scientist's ownership of a scientific text, a poet's inscription in a volume of verse, a historian's notes in a historical chronicle — these create dialogues across time.

The relationship between owner and object matters as much as the name itself.

A volume from a great library can also carry inherent weight. The shelves of a thoughtful collector reflect years of thoughtful deliberation. To acquire a book from such a library is, in a small way, to inherit a fragment of that journey.

There is a difference between a famous name and a meaningful one. The market rewards the former; seasoned collectors appreciate the latter.

At its best, provenance does not simply increase price — it increases presence. The book feels situated in human history rather than floating outside it.

The most compelling provenance does not shout a name; it tells a story.

The Poetry of Ordinary Ownership

There is also refined beauty in modest provenance.

A 19th-century school prize inscription.

A family name written carefully on a flyleaf.

A date marking when a book entered a household.

These do not always increase market value, but they humanize the object. A book does not need celebrity to possess history.

When Provenance Softens Condition

A book with meaningful provenance may forgive flaws that would trouble a lesser copy.

Wear may be accepted as the cost of a documented life. An inscription may outweigh a stain. A historically important association can reframe what collectors are willing to overlook.

Context, once again, governs judgment.

Many seasoned collectors eventually confess that they are drawn not only to fine copies, but to interesting ones.

The two are not always the same.

Recording the Chain

Thoughtful collectors document provenance as they acquire books.

A note of purchase, a retained catalog description, a remembered story from a seller — these become part of the book's continuing record.

In doing so, the collector becomes not only a recipient of history, but a contributor to it.

The chain does not end; it lengthens.

A Moment of Realization

One collector recalls opening a newly acquired volume and noticing, almost by accident, a faint inscription on the flyleaf. The ink had softened with age, the strokes slightly uneven, as though written with care rather than haste.

It recorded a gift between siblings, offered more than a century earlier. Only a brief line accompanied it — a simple expression of affection and a date written in a steady hand.

Nothing about the inscription altered the book's market value. It was not an author's signature, nor a notable name. By commercial standards, it was incidental.

Yet the moment invited pause.

Here was evidence that the book had once been chosen deliberately, wrapped perhaps, presented with intention. It had marked an occasion in someone's life — a birthday, a holiday, a farewell. The giver and receiver were long gone, their circumstances unknowable, their relationship reduced to a few words in fading ink.

And still, the gesture endured.

The collector found himself lingering over the page longer than expected. The book no longer felt like a solitary artifact; it felt like the remainder of a human exchange, a small bridge between ordinary lives separated by time.

One realizes, in such moments, that books are not only read — they are given, carried, kept, and remembered. They pass through affections as well as through hands.

A faint inscription can outlive the moment that inspired it, and in doing so, lend that moment a second life.

The Moment of Holding

Late afternoon light entered the shop at a shallow angle, illuminating the upper shelves while the lower rows remained in shade. The air held the settled scent of paper and old wood — dry, composed, faintly mineral.

The bookseller returned carrying a parcel wrapped in brown paper and tied with thin string. He did not speak as he set it down. The knot was loosened with practiced fingers. The paper folded back.

The book remained closed for a breath.

Its weight settled first — neither heavy nor slight, but proportioned. Boards firm. The cloth at the extremities softened by years of contact. Lettering dulled just enough to prove it had lived honestly. The spine showed a natural arc, not fatigue.

Instinct directs the hands before the eye fully engages. Structure first.

The volume was opened gently at the midpoint, not to read, but to listen through the fingertips. The hinges yielded without strain. The sewing held. The text block flexed and returned.

Only then did the title page receive attention.

The date once marked the present tense of its printing. Beneath it, an inscription in ink now browned by decades: a name, a place, a year written in a hand both careful and assured. No famous association. No catalog distinction. Only evidence that someone, somewhere, had once regarded this volume as worth inscribing.

The pages turned evenly. Margins remained broad. The paper, faintly toned, retained resilience. A slight darkening along the fore-edge suggested years near light, but not neglect. The sewing at the inner margin held firm — visible, intact, sufficient.

In such moments, terminology recedes.

Edition. Issue. Scarcity. Market.

Recognition replaces vocabulary.

The description becomes the object. The imagined copy becomes the one held.

There is no triumph — only alignment.

The covers close with deliberation. The text block settles cleanly. Nothing resists.

The bookseller waits without pressure.

The decision, when it arrives, feels less like acquisition than acceptance.

The paper is drawn back into place. The string is retied, firm but not tight. The parcel rests briefly between seller and buyer — suspended between past and future.

Outside, the light has shifted again.

The book leaves with you.

What happens next will depend on how you keep it.

CHAPTER VI

On the Habits and Heart of a Collector

The Slow Education of Taste

No one begins as a finished collector.

Taste, in books as in art, is not declared — it is developed.
It forms gradually through exposure, comparison, and

reflection. A book admired early in one's journey may later feel ordinary; another once overlooked may grow in appeal.

This evolution is not inconsistency but refinement.

Collectors discover that their libraries trace a map of their changing interests. Shelves become a record not only of acquisitions, but of intellectual growth. A mature collection rarely appears all at once. It reveals itself gradually.

The Discipline of Restraint

Restraint is not the enemy of enthusiasm.

To decline a book can be as meaningful as to acquire one. Every thoughtful collector eventually learns that saying "not this copy" is part of saying "yes" to a better one later.

The market rewards judgement more reliably than speed.

Restraint also preserves joy. A library assembled without measure can begin to feel like inventory. A library assembled with intention remains a source of delight.

Some collectors pursue authors. Others pursue eras, bindings, themes, or histories. Some follow a thread so personal it is visible only to them. Focus lends coherence. It transforms accumulation into curation.

A small, thoughtful collection reveals more about its owner than a large, indiscriminate one. The former suggests attention, the latter, appetite. Neither is wrong, but one tends to endure.

The Interior Reward

The deepest rewards of collecting are often private. A solitary hour spent revisiting one's shelves. The recognition of a well-chosen copy. The memory of where and why a book was acquired.

These satisfactions do not appear in auction results or catalog descriptions, yet they sustain the practice.

A library can become a form of autobiography written in bindings and paper.

The Company of Books

Books offer a particular kind of companionship.

They do not hurry, compete, or demand. They wait with a patience few other objects possess. A book may sit unopened for years and yet receive its reader without reproach when returned to.

There is an abiding generosity in this.

A library grows not only as a collection of texts, but as a gathering of presences. Certain volumes become familiar by sight alone — their spines recognized like old acquaintances, their places on the shelf remembered without conscious effort.

Collectors find that they live among their books as much as they live with them. A shelf passed daily becomes a landscape of remembered interests: the period one studied exploration, the year devoted to Victorian fiction, the season when illustrated books held fascination.

In this way, a library begins to mirror an interior life.

Books also accompany us through change. The same volume opened at twenty may feel different at forty, though the words remain fixed. The reader shifts, the book endures. The dialogue between them continues across time.

Some collectors find that the comfort of a library lies not only in what has been read, but in what remains possible. Unread books do not accuse; they invite.

A room lined with books carries a distinctive calm. It suggests stored thought, deferred conversation, and the presence of many minds at rest.

To sit among books is, in a sense, to keep company with centuries.

CHAPTER VII

Living With Books: The Private Life of a Collection

A book's life does not end when it is purchased. It begins there.

Much has been written about how to find books, evaluate them, and acquire them wisely. Far less is said about what follows — the long, quiet companionship that unfolds after a book joins a home.

Collecting is not only the pursuit of books; it is the experience of living among them.

A personal library exerts a subtle influence. Shelves shape rooms, and rooms shape habits. A book left within reach is more likely to be opened. A familiar spine glimpsed in passing can recall a forgotten idea, a passage, a memory of when it was first read.

Books do not demand engagement. They wait. Yet their presence quietly alters the atmosphere of a space. A room lined with books rarely feels empty, even in solitude.

Over time, a collection becomes less a set of possessions than an environment — a landscape of thought, interest, and curiosity rendered in paper and binding.

The Arrangement of a Mind

No two libraries are arranged alike.

Some collectors organize by subject, others by chronology, others by size or binding. Some arrange meticulously; others allow organic groupings to form. There is no single correct method, because every arrangement reflects a way of thinking.

A shelf devoted to exploration may sit beside one devoted to childhood favorites. Fine bindings may coexist with modest paperbacks kept for sentimental reasons. A library

reveals priorities that even its owner may not fully
articulate.

To browse one's own shelves is to rediscover past selves
— earlier interests, former fascinations, phases of study
and enthusiasm. Books purchased years apart converse
silently with one another.

In this way, a collection becomes a map of intellectual life,
drawn gradually rather than designed at once.

The Books Kept for Oneself

Not every book in a collection is acquired for display or
status.

Some are kept for reasons that resist explanation: a
childhood edition that first sparked wonder, a battered
copy found during a meaningful trip, a volume associated
with a season of life. Their market value may be modest;
their personal value may be immeasurable.

Collectors speak more readily about rare acquisitions than
about these private volumes. Yet it is the latter that would
be hardest to part with.

These books form the spirit of a library — the portion
shaped by memory rather than market.

They remind us that collecting is not purely an economic activity. It is also an emotional and intellectual one.

Returning to the Shelf

An interesting change occurs as a collection matures.

Early on, the excitement lies in acquisition. Later, satisfaction comes from revisiting what is already owned. A collector may pull a volume from the shelf not to inspect it, but simply to read a passage again or to admire its construction.

Ownership becomes familiarity. Familiarity becomes relationship.

A well-loved library is not static. Books are shifted, opened, reconsidered. Some are moved to more prominent places; others recede but remain valued. The collection evolves along with its owner.

Living with books, then, is an ongoing dialogue rather than a completed project.

A Library as a Lived Space

A personal library does not need to resemble an institution to hold meaning. It may occupy a single bookcase, a study, or several rooms. Its importance lies not in scale but in intention.

Books absorb the rhythms of the household. They exist near conversations, daily routines, and moments of reflection. A child pulling a volume from a lower shelf, a guest pausing to read a title aloud, a familiar book opened on a quiet evening in a reading nook — these small interactions give a collection its life.

A library that is used, even gently, feels more alive than one kept behind glass.

The collector who lives with books, rather than merely storing them, experiences them as part of daily life rather than as distant artifacts.

What Lies Ahead

A collector may wonder what will become of the library in the distant future. Such thoughts are natural, but they need not overshadow the present.

The first purpose of a personal collection is not legacy, but living. Books are meant to be handled, read, revisited, and enjoyed in their time with us. Their deeper significance lies in how they shape the days in which they are present.

There is a quiet temptation to think always in terms of posterity — of inheritance, dispersal, auction, or donation.

Shelves begin to resemble archives of consequence rather than companions of daily life. Yet a library gathered for its future risks neglecting its present. A book unopened for fear of diminishing its condition may remain preserved, but it is not fully possessed.

The truest life of a collection unfolds in ordinary moments: a volume pulled down on a winter evening, a passage reread after years, a marginal note rediscovered that reveals who we once were. The value of such experiences cannot be appraised, yet they are often the most enduring return on the investment of time and attention.

Collections may be inherited, dispersed, donated, or divided. Some volumes will travel into other hands; others may find homes in institutions; still others will continue their steady migration through the marketplace. This is not loss but continuation. Books have always moved from reader to reader, shelf to shelf.

If a library one day passes on, let it do so as something that was genuinely lived with — not merely accumulated. The true measure of a collection is not how impressively it concludes, but how fully it accompanied the life that assembled it.

In the end, the future of the library matters less than the presence of it. What lies ahead will unfold beyond our keeping. What lies here now, on the shelf within reach, is ours to open.

CHAPTER VIII

Modern Tools, Timeless Judgment

On AI and the Contemporary Collector

Old Pursuit, New Instruments

Rare-book collecting is an old pursuit.

For centuries, collectors relied on dealers' catalogs, bibliographies, correspondence, and personal networks. Knowledge traveled slowly, and judgment developed through handling, comparison, and conversation.

Today, information travels differently. Databases compile auction records, digital archives make texts searchable, and artificial intelligence can summarize, compare, and retrieve information in moments.

These are new instruments in an old practice.

Their presence does not change the nature of collecting, but it does change how collectors prepare themselves.

The Promise of Assistance

AI excels at gathering and organizing information.

It can:

- Surface past auction results
- Compare editions
- Summarize bibliographic references
- Help identify points of issue
- Provide historical context quickly

For a collector beginning research, this can be invaluable. What once required weeks of correspondence or travel can now begin in minutes.

Access to information has widened the doorway into the field.

This is a genuine gift to modern collectors.

The Limits of Automation

Information alone is not judgment. An algorithm can list prices, but it cannot feel paper. It can summarize editions, but it cannot sense a strained hinge. It can retrieve history, but it cannot perceive presence.

A book's appeal lies in subtleties: tone of cloth, impression of type, balance of margins, the natural authority of an unrestored copy.

These are apprehended by eye and hand, not by database.

Collectors who rely solely on digital knowledge may know much about books without fully knowing books themselves.

Technology excels at aggregation. It gathers records, compares sales, and organizes data at a scale no individual could manage. This capacity is valuable. It broadens access and shortens research time. Many collectors today learn faster because of it.

But databases describe patterns, not particulars. They speak in averages and histories, while every physical copy carries its own reality. Two books of the same edition may share a record yet differ greatly when placed side by side.

Automation also lacks context for nuance. A listing might note "minor wear," yet the character of that wear — its visibility, its placement, its effect on appearance — remains outside numerical language. A crease at the spine head tells a different story than one at the fore-edge, though both may be summarized similarly.

There is also the matter of aesthetic response. Some books possess a harmony of design that becomes evident only when held: proportions that feel balanced, typography that rests easily on the page, materials that age gracefully. Such qualities resist quantification.

Digital tools can indicate what a book *is*. They cannot fully convey what a book *feels like*.

This distinction matters most as one advances in collecting. Early on, data provides orientation. Later, perception guides choice. The seasoned collector does not abandon research but supplements it with direct experience.

Technology, then, functions best as an instrument rather than a substitute. It informs, but it does not decide. It narrows the field, but it does not complete the evaluation.

Books remain physical artifacts. Their presence occupies space, carries texture, and interacts with light. These qualities live beyond the reach of code.

The most satisfying collections arise from a partnership between knowledge and encounter — where research prepares the mind, and direct engagement confirms the choice.

Automation can point toward a book. Only the collector can recognize when it truly belongs on the shelf.

In medicine, algorithms assist but do not decide. A clinical tool may flag a lab value, calculate risk, or suggest a protocol, yet it cannot perceive the subtle hesitations in a patient's voice, the posture that betrays fatigue, or the instinctive recognition that something is not quite right. Data informs judgment; it does not replace it. The experienced physician reads beyond the numbers, weighing context, history, and the quiet evidence of encounter. Collecting operates in much the same way. A database can list auction records, summarize editions, and quantify rarity, but it cannot register the authority of an unrestored spine, the harmony of proportion on a well-set page, or the quiet conviction that a particular copy simply feels right. Algorithms reveal patterns; collectors interpret the particular. In both fields, tools widen vision — but discernment remains human.

Pattern and Perspective

AI is particularly useful for revealing patterns.

It can show how frequently a title appears, how prices fluctuate, how editions differ in description. Such perspective helps temper impulse and ground expectations.

Patterns reveal the landscape; they do not describe the terrain underfoot.

A record of past sales can suggest a typical range, yet it cannot explain why one copy surpassed another. A higher result may reflect superior presentation, provenance, timing, or simple competition between determined bidders. The numbers alone rarely tell the full story.

Frequency data also requires interpretation. A book that surfaces frequently may indicate abundance — or it may reflect active trading among collectors. A title that appears rarely may signal scarcity — or merely limited recent demand. Context gives meaning to recurrence.

AI can also highlight textual differences between editions with impressive speed. It can collate publication details, identify variant points, and summarize bibliographic distinctions. This capability saves hours of manual comparison.

Yet bibliographic similarity does not guarantee equivalence in appeal. Two editions may share content but differ in design, materials, or visual presence. Collectors respond to these qualities instinctively, even when the differences seem slight on paper.

There is also the matter of timing. Market patterns reflect the past more than the present. A surge of interest in a particular author or genre can shift values quickly. Historical data provides guidance, but not certainty.

Collectors who use AI effectively treat it as orientation. It maps the broader market, highlights anomalies, and prompts questions. The final judgment still rests with the individual.

Perspective, after all, depends on more than scale. It depends on interpretation.

Pattern recognition is a powerful aid. It becomes wisdom only when paired with human evaluation.

The Collector's Role

The thoughtful collector remains the final interpreter.

AI can widen the field of view, but it cannot decide what is meaningful, beautiful, or worth preserving. Those judgments remain human.

Collecting has always blended knowledge with intuition. Modern tools expand the knowledge; they do not replace the intuition.

A balanced collector uses technology as a lantern, not a compass.

Continuity, Not Disruption

Every generation has adopted new tools.

Printed bibliographies once replaced handwritten lists.

Photographic catalogs once supplemented written descriptions.

Online databases once replaced printed records.

AI belongs to this lineage of aids.

The heart of collecting — curiosity, patience, discernment, stewardship — remains unchanged.

The book in hand is still the final authority.

Technology can accelerate learning, but it cannot shorten experience. A collector's eye still develops slowly, shaped by comparison, conversation, and time.

The wisest use of modern tools is not to replace the old ways, but to support them.

In the end, even in a digital age, the collector's truest education still arrives page by page, and book by book.

CHAPTER IX

On Joy, Meaning, and the Life of a Collector

The Quiet Motive

People wonder why collectors collect.

The question is usually posed in terms of price or prestige, yet most collectors recognize that these are only partial explanations. The deeper motive is more subtle, personal, and difficult to name.

A collector seldom pursues books for possession alone. More often, they are seeking connection — to history, to language, to the lingering life of ideas. Books provide a tangible thread between past and present, thought and touch, memory and meaning.

Selecting a volume that speaks to one's curiosity carries private satisfaction. The choice may appear small, yet it reflects an inward inclination, a private pattern of passion forming over time.

The motive, then, is not merely acquisition, but affinity — a desire to dwell near the durable expressions of human thought.

Many collectors, if pressed, might admit that the pleasure lies less in owning than in recognizing: recognizing a work that matters to them, recognizing a connection to a period or person, recognizing themselves in the shape of their shelves.

Interest deepens into attachment, and attachment into belonging.

The Silent Joy of the Hunt

There is a particular pleasure known only to those who search for books with intention.

The hunt is rarely hurried. It unfolds in catalog pages turned slowly, in shelves scanned with a practiced eye, in listings revisited more than once before a decision is made. Much of it occurs in silence, guided by curiosity rather than urgency.

The joy lies not solely in discovery, but in anticipation. A collector learns to enjoy the looking as much as the finding — the comparison of copies, the weighing of condition, the small spark of recognition when a desirable example appears.

Some searches last weeks; others last years. A long pursuit can lend a book a kind of gravity before it is ever acquired. By the time it is found, the collector already knows its shape in the mind.

Even near misses refine the eye.

At its best, the hunt is contemplative. It rewards attentiveness, patience, and memory. It invites the collector to move deliberately through possibility.

Over time, one realizes that the pursuit itself becomes part of the reward. The stories of where a book was found, how long it was sought, and what was learned along the way will outlast the thrill of the purchase.

The finest finds are those that have first taken time to be sought.

A Personal Library as Reflection

Even when assembled gradually, a library gathers around
the contours of a life. Certain subjects recur, certain
authors reappear, certain eras hold attention longer than
others. Patterns emerge that the collector may not
consciously design, yet they reveal themselves all the same.

A library becomes an unintended autobiography, written in
bindings rather than ink.

Seen this way, a collection is less an archive of paper than a
map of attention. A collection traces a mind in motion.
Books record who we have been as much as they record
what we have read.

Visitors notice these patterns before the collector does.
They read the shelves as one might read marginalia —
glimpsing the outline of a mind through its selections.

Libraries also preserve earlier versions of ourselves. The
book purchased in youth remains even when tastes mature.
The once-beloved subject that no longer commands focus
still occupies its place, a reminder of prior fascinations.

A library, therefore, is not static. It is layered. It contains
the record of who the collector has been as well as who
they are becoming.

To stand before one's shelves can be to survey an unspoken autobiography written without intention, yet rich with implication.

In the end, a personal library is less a display of books than a portrait of a life in thought.

Permission to Collect What You Love

Collectors look outward for validation. Not every pleasure requires defense.

There is joy in finding a copy that feels right — in the texture of old cloth, the elegance of type, the surprise of a well-preserved jacket. These satisfactions may appear small to others, but to a collector they carry genuine meaning.

Joy in collecting need not be rationalized as investment or scholarship; it may exist purely as appreciation.

A book chosen with delight remains memorable long after its price is forgotten.

Over time, many seasoned collectors arrive at a simple realization: the most meaningful libraries are shaped not by consensus, but by affection.

A book that genuinely delights its owner will be opened, revisited, remembered. A book acquired solely for reputation may remain admired yet distant, like a painting hung for guests rather than for oneself.

Collecting, at its best, is not a performance but a relationship — a long conversation between curiosity and care.

There is a particular freedom in allowing one's interests to be personal. To collect a minor author because their work speaks to you, to pursue a narrow subject because it holds your attention, to value a modest book because it carries private significance — these choices lend a library character and sincerity.

Taste matures not by imitation, but by attention.

Some of the most distinctive collections were built by individuals who trusted their fascinations more than prevailing fashion. Their shelves reflected genuine engagement, and that authenticity gave their libraries coherence.

The Company One Keeps

The phrase *the company one keeps* is used for people, yet it applies just as naturally to books.

A personal library becomes, over years, a circle of chosen voices. Historians, poets, novelists, printers, illustrators — all gathered in silent proximity. Their words rest side by side, their thoughts separated by centuries yet meeting on the same shelves.

To live among books is to live among brilliant minds.

There is a subtle comfort in this presence. Even in silence, it suggests stored conversation, deferred discovery, and the reassuring weight of accumulated thought.

Certain books grow companionable simply by duration. Their spines soften, their positions on the shelf become instinctive. One knows where they reside without looking, the way one remembers the seat of a longtime acquaintance at a table.

Over a lifetime, the library becomes a gathering of influences. The authors who shaped one's thinking, the subjects that stirred curiosity, the works that offered consolation or challenge — all remain pervasive over time.

We do not merely keep books; they keep something of us as well. They hold the memory of who we were when we first opened them, and they receive us again when we return changed.

A collector's shelves therefore become more than storage. They form a kind of society — a silent fellowship of ideas and imaginations that accompany a life without demanding it.

No Final Arrival

Collectors sometimes imagine a moment of completion.

A certain number of volumes, a finished author set, a shelf that finally feels full — each can create the illusion of arrival. Yet most who collect for long discover that the sense of completion is fleeting.

Interests shift. New questions arise. What once absorbed us may quietly give way to something new. The library expands not only outward on its shelves, but inward in its meaning.

To accept that a collection remains open-ended is to allow it to remain alive.

Some of the greatest pleasure in collecting lies precisely in this incompletion. The possibility of future discovery keeps the pursuit vibrant. The next catalog, the next conversation, the next unexpected encounter — all hold potential. Libraries, like lives, move in seasons. Periods of gathering alternate with periods of reflection.

The shelves remain.

Closing Reflection - On the Enduring Life of Books and Those Who Keep Them

In the end, collecting is a modest act in a hurried world.

It asks us to slow down — to notice paper and type, to care about the survival of small things. A collector spends time with objects made to outlast their moment, and in doing so adopts a longer view of time itself.

Books remind us that ideas outlast circumstance. Hands change; pages remain. What is carefully kept today may speak to someone not yet conceived.

A personal library, whether small or expansive, is never merely a possession. It is a record of attention — a gathering of what one has chosen to value.

No collector keeps books forever. One keeps them well for a while.

The shelves we build will one day be sorted by other hands, read by other eyes, and continued in ways we cannot foresee. Our role is simple: to choose thoughtfully, to care attentively, and to pass along what we have preserved.

And perhaps that is enough.

A life among books teaches that meaning rarely arrives in grand gestures. It gathers in quiet decisions: a book saved, a note kept, a volume chosen because it stirred curiosity or wonder.

In time, those small acts become something larger than ownership.

Long after we are gone, a book we once held may open
beneath another reader's hand.

And when it does, the work continues.

Acknowledgments

No collection is built alone, and no collector learns in isolation.

I am grateful first to my family, whose patience and encouragement make room for both books and the time they require. A home that welcomes books is a home that welcomes curiosity, memory, and conversation. Their support gently sustains this work more than they know.

I owe thanks as well to the many booksellers, collectors, and scholars who share their knowledge generously. Those who trade in rare books trade in stories too, and their willingness to answer questions, explain details, and pass along insight keeps the culture of collecting alive. Much of what any collector learns comes from listening to those who have handled more books and made more mistakes.

I am also indebted to the long tradition of bibliophiles whose writings and collections shaped the field before my time. Every modern collector benefits from a lineage of careful observers who valued preservation and thoughtful description.

Any wisdom in these pages is drawn from shared knowledge and experience; any shortcomings remain my own.

www.ingramcontent.com/pod-product-compliance
Lightning Source LLC
Chambersburg PA
CBHW051445140726

47987CB00006B/2553